Duncan Forbes was born in 194[...]
His poems have appeared in the [...]
Spectator and the *Times Literary S[...]*
a Gregory Award. His first colle[...]
published by Secker & Warburg in 1984 and he won 1st Prize
in the *TLS* / Blackwells Poetry Competition in 1998. His
previous Enitharmon books have been *Public & Confidential*
(1989), *Taking Liberties* (1993) and *Voice Mail* (2002).

*For Kath
with love and in
honour of the wonderful
Tender Age experience
x x x*

Duncan Forbes

Vision Mixer

ENITHARMON PRESS

First published in 2006
by the Enitharmon Press
26B Caversham Road
London NW5 2DU

www.enitharmon.co.uk

Distributed in the UK by
Central Books
99 Wallis Road
London E9 5LN

Distributed in the USA and Canada
by Dufour Editions Inc.
PO Box 7, Chester Springs
PA 19425, USA

© Duncan Forbes 2006

ISBN 1 904634 15 X

Enitharmon Press gratefully acknowledges the financial support of
Arts Council England, London.

British Library Cataloguing-in-Publication Data.
A catalogue record for this book is available
from the British Library.

Typeset in Bembo by Servis Filmsetting Ltd
and printed in England by
Antony Rowe Ltd

Contents

Old Master 9
Second Childhood 10
Climbing My Father 11
Old Man 12
80 14
Mental Health Act 15
Demonized 16
Food Chain 17
Neuropathology 18
Absconditus 19
Meditation 20
Process 21
R.S.V.P. 22
Theocracy 23
Do You Want to Put God in the Recycle Bin? 24
A Dictionary of Walking Misquotations 25
Dear John 26
Horses 28
God Glances at *The Life of Mammals* 29
Blackbird at Dusk 32
Credo 33
Reasons to Wake 34
Mute Swan 38
Wasp 39
Minutes 40
Horticulturalist 41
David Kennedy 42
Posidonio 44
Seed Head 45
Day-Trip 46
Do Not Disturb 47
Decent Citizen 48
Theory 49
September Birthdays 50
Hymn to Pimm's 51
In the Vendée. Remember? 52
Indoor Market 53
Leopard 54
Tomorrow 55
Lycoperdon 56
History of Tom 57
All Saints 59
Anthropophily 61
Guilt 62
Telephone 63
International Gallery 65
Sheriff of Washington 71
Sir John Betjeman Turns in His Grave 73
Risk Assessment 75
Autumn Again 76
Brown Dragonfly 77
Toad 78
Bubbly 79
Sex Romp in Head's Garden 80
Flight 81
God 83
Friday Night with Jonathan Ross 84
Sloe Gin 85
Window Seat 86

8 October 87
Winter Weather 88
August Bank Holiday 89
Struthio 90
Tonight 91
Sleep 92
God in the Small Hours 93
Patriarch 94
Outlook 95
Typography 96
Magpie 97
In the Cupboard 98

Mother and Daughter 99
An Odyssey 100
Tanga 101
Denial 102
Garden Leave 104
Gifts 105
Round 106
Sands 107
Mystic 108
Vision 109
Whodunnit 110
Full Circle 112

Acknowledgements

Acknowledgements and special thanks are due to the editors of the following publications in which some of these poems first appeared:

Ambit, Acumen, Agenda, Areté, Brittle Star, Dandelion, Equinox, Inclement, London Magazine, Poetry Monthly, Peterloo Poets Competition Anthology, The Interpreter's House, Understanding.

Old Master

God took up painting again.
It was more difficult than ever to create a masterpiece
and where should the oldest of masters begin
now that there was also the problem of belatedness,
as well as the new techniques and the critics?
Painting is Dead. God is Dead. They said, they said.
Well, he would prove them wrong himself.
Look, look around at my installations,
the kinetic verve of my constellations,
the videos of my action paintings,
the fluid sculptures in the clouds
and watercolours on every ocean,
but all the self-portraits shook their heads.
They wanted to be the gods instead.

Second Childhood

He's grown a beard and looks like Jeremiah
In his pyjamas but as biddable
As a young child or more so, to be fair.
Though much of what he says is verbal scribble,
He can respond to music and old friends
But can't remember where his radio is
Or how to switch it on and tune the dial.
He walks with the assistance of a stick
And often answers 'don't know' or pretends.
His medic's memory, once formidable,
Has disappeared into the brain's abyss.
Of all the things I showed him on our walk,
He liked the spring lambs best: white herbivores
Practising vertical take-off on all fours.

Climbing My Father

The egg-timer releases upside down
A fraying thread of rusty-coloured sand.
We're in the kitchen underneath the clothes rack
Hung with Sea Island Cotton underpants
Which seem gigantic, he a giant too.
Hands in his helping hands, feet on his knees,
I clamber up the stomach muscles' wall,
Cross wobbly areas of wincing flesh
Up to his chest, fling legs across his shoulders,
Until eureka I am looking down
On fluffy hair and suntan on the summit.
The clothes rack on a pulley now in reach,
He lowers me from ceiling to the ground.
The eggs are boiled. And mountains washed to sand.

Old Man

I was not always here,
a helpless paralysed man,
bald and gone in the teeth.
I boxed and swam for the school,
rowed in the Boat Race twice,
a wartime rugby blue,
I won a medal in Nice
and looked like a film star once,
a tall dark handsome youth,
not this cadaverous dunce
whose musculature has gone
and whose mind is not all there.

A former connoisseur
of food and vintage wine,
I drink from a carton of juice
you say is a favourite of mine
now that I dribble and grin,
then breathe a sigh of despair
with pineapple juice on my chin.
You feed me as if I'm a child,
you bath me with flannel and soap
but the words I think run wild
so I wink instead in the hope
I might mean what you guess.

And the grandchildren? I confess
I can't remember their names
nor how many there are.
Brothers, two sisters and twins,
you show me their photographs
in an album of colourful scenes
and I play along with the game
but the mind can no longer induce
obstinate tongue to speak
things I want it to voice
and, paralysed in the brain,
the unheard memories stick.

So what do you see in my face?
Lines where I frowned and laughed?
An old decrepit man
broken by eighty years,
no memories fore and aft?
I smile as if it's a dream,
this ageing process lark,
and not an unbearable fight
against frustration and pain
but sometimes I want to scream:
Put out the overhead dark
and leave me alone in the light.

80

It is his birthday and the two old men
embrace and hug, their cheeks not touching, then
they part and hold each other, looking into eyes
octogenarian and young again
as if at the imponderable surprise
that they should be empirically alive
towards the end of their own lifetimes.

'My dear old friend,' says Peter weighing words
which Alec now can only smile towards.
They touch and it is touching, move and moving.
Contemporaries at school and college friends,
both are more sentimental now and loving
as if they held the present of each other
against their non-existence altogether.

Mental Health Act

Only a legal eagle could divide
The person from the purse-strings and decide
How much the family hopes should be denied.
For the purpose of this law a person is
Divisible into legal and financial.
It doesn't matter whether damages
To persons and emotions are substantial.

You did not know he'd fallen in the garden
And was in hospital with a transection
Until we told you of your ignorance
Which daily grows more difficult to pardon.
The mind is angry and the mood aggrieves.
Dear Mistrust Office, Court of Self-protection,
Have you read *Bleak House* and/or *Falling Leaves*?

Demonized

A nightmare face. The Bette Davis role.
The gingko earrings made of abalone
On grinning monkey mask with black moustache.
The floral trousers on a chimpanzee
With toad-like figure and clipped Kiwi vowels.
The horror-movie grasping second wife
Whose sudden switch from saccharine to harsh
Marks wicked stepmother who wants control.

What are her motives? Hatred and revenge,
Power and possession? Love and lovelessness?
The pension fund? Low cunning? Cultural cringe?
What turned her into such a sociopath?
Dear Satan, are you female and if so
What is your Christian name? I think I know.

Food Chain

And have you ever had C-J Disease?
Or bovine spongiform encephalopathy?
Are you aware of scrapie now in sheep?
The prions spread into the spinal cord
And murder other cells. Have you endured,
O ultimate in doctors and degrees,
Leukodepletion of your precious blood?
Conventional filtration intercepts
Some 99% bacteria but
10 millilitres of infected blood
Can cause an international epidemic.
For what emergencies do you lose sleep?
I'm sorry, sir, to nag you and to moan
But do you ever check your answerphone?

Neuropathology

Patients with cortical Lewy body disease
will often suffer from severe dementia and
may earlier on display a fluctuating
course to their illness and may suffer from
persistent (visual) hallucinations . . .
as well as evidence of Parkinson's
and of a cortical dementia with
aphasia, agnosia and apraxia.
Cortical Lewy bodies are particularly
numerous in cingulate or insular
and parahippocampal cortices.
In other words, it's difficult to speak,
to think conceptually or to act,
those three new destinies from ancient Greek.

Absconditus

Have you not in your infinite wisdom heard,
O God of love, paterfamilias,
the GOYA principle? (Get Off Your Arse).
You're looking like a kingsize absent nerd.
Have you deserted your paternal post
and are you stuck out somewhere near Infinity
discussing physics with the Holy Ghost,
contiguous universes and the Trinity?
We've made a breeding, feeding, bleeding mess
of what was once an earthly Paradise,
a prelapsarian Eden, more or less,
and need your help before we blow it twice.
What we find shocking is your unconcern
for us, your children, who will never learn.

Meditation

Dear God, are you a transcendentalist
and can you also seem to rise above it?
If people get your goat or miss the gist
do you just turn the other cheek and love it?
Or do you clench one godalmighty fist
and tell them in as many words to shove it?

The trees, the sun, the sea, the sky, the mist,
the ocean's depth, the mountain's elevation,
the way that shark and tiger co-exist:
does nature satisfy your contemplation,
not in the spirit of a narcissist
because you're looking at your own creation,
or do you need that freakshow humankind
to complicate things with its petty mind?

Process

My tits grow pendulous and rather pappy
Under a silverfront of grizzled grey.
A dot moves like a cursor on the page
And small print is a blur in any light.
My standards grow more sloppy and slap-happy.
The broad mind and the narrow waist changed places
Some years ago but seems like yesterday.
What is no longer muscle but a belly
Came here to stay one Christmas. Never left.
My memory fails me now for names and faces.
I sleep more easily all times of day –
Just plonk me on a sofa, watching telly –
And press-ups (ten a day – well, that's a lie)
Get harder and slower as the years flop by.

R.S.V.P.

Before I trust, as to a lover's tryst,
My psyche to your archetypal power,
Dear God, are you a psychoanalyst
And how much if so do you charge an hour?
Are you a healer on the National Health?
Are you a Jungian or a Zionist?
Do you believe in free association
And are you mystic or behaviourist?
Répondez s'il vous plaît to this oblation,
Herr Doktor Gott, whatever your persuasion,
Or do you take me for an egotist
Whose rambling monologue talking to itself
Is my attempt at atheistic prayer,
A manifesto of innate despair?

THEOCRACY

O Dad of donnée, data, all that's given,
Your majesty, our feudal lord in heaven,
Your wish is our command both here and there.

Give us our daily modicum of food
And do not take us to the moral cleaners
For major or for minor misdemeanours,
As we forgive those who forget a feud.

Please don't seduce us with temptation's dare
But keep us on the narrow straight and level,
With no remission for a devious devil.

Omnipotence and glory hallelujah
Are yours as long as always has a future,
Since you're the boss, King God, the grand panjandrum
Of random balls. *Quod erat demonstrandum.*

Do You Want to Put God in the Recycle Bin?

right mister right mister right mister right.
Dear god of particle acceleration
and landlord of infinity and night
inventor of equations and creation
engenderer of gender differences
the artist-dreamer and supreme creator
of superstrings and other galaxies,
dear astrophysical predestinator,
have you a website and dot com address?
What search engine would open up your portals?
How can a hacker calculate or guess?
Please listen sometimes though we are mere mortals.
We aren't all einsteins newtons aristotles
but dodos sending messages in bottles

A Dictionary of Walking Misquotations

There is more enterprise in walking naked
Though life is not a stroll across a field;
You cannot fertilize it with a fart.
Tears, idle tears, I know not if they mean
The course of true love never did run smooth.
Sunt lacrimae rerum. You have to laugh.
Hope springs eternal in the human breast
But there's no ship to take me from myself,
Time will say nothing but I told you so
To justify the ways of God to man
Or vice versa – all is relative,
Reality can't bear much humankind
But *Eli, Eli, lama sabachtani*
And so say all of us. The rest is silence.

Dear John

John Henry Franklin Eminson
(1956–1998)

I remember the pints of beer,
your acumen and fluent pen,
your civil servant's admin mind,
mental arithmetic no fear,
faster than a calculator,
your terrier-like tenacity,
the Billy Bremner of a team,
your dress-sense and the man-made fibres,
your unswerving loyal support
of losing and lost causes like
Doncaster Rovers (never say die),
your justice and integrity,
a right-hand man in bunker days,
your boyishly paternal pride
in Mark and Charlotte, then in Tom,
and your judicious words of praise,
your love of literature and sport,
the population of each novel,
the poet's personalities
and the inhabitants of plays
since it was people who make days
for the would-be football journalist
who married in his Oxford phase,
protective of the underdog,
the misfit's mentor with a true
relish of individuals –
why has it taken me so long
to choose these words to say of you?

Because of all those troubled years?
The ailing mother in a home,
the marriage moving to divorce,
the mind not stable and the grim
'Duncan, you do not understand
how truly desolate it is,
the blankness of a blank despair',
the therapy ('she has your eyes')
and loneliness which drink disguised.
What chemical imbalance or
disturbance of a troubled mind
led you one morning and your car
to the hard shoulder out to find
a death which could not swerve in time?
It was unlike your better self
to bother someone else and leave
a family of four to grieve.

Agnostically, I hope you saw
the chapel full of people who
loved you for what you meant and were
and in that coffin as you lay
or else inanimate at last
I wish your troubled spirit rest.
And I remember one good friend
say in the crematorium
that anyone who really knew
could never fail to love you too.
We could not understand both why
and how it was you had to die.
I speak as if you still exist
and you could listen to me try.
Ah well, dear John, you always were
a sympathetic listener.

Horses

The grazing horses walked towards the fence,
beckoned by the open hand of green
horse chestnut fingers in my human hand.
We had to put some barbed wire on the fence
because they scratched their bums and leant against it.
Three of the horses had new foals beside them,
tall frisky baby versions of their mothers.
One newborn had long eyelashes and white whiskers.
Another suckled from her mother's teats.
The dappled grey was pregnant as a barrel;
We thought she'd drop her foal at any time.
Last year one foaled right here beside the fence
and we two watched her from our bedrooom window.
The other horses also stood and watched
and when the foal was born they did a dance
around the mother and their newborn child
which could stand up and run within the hour.
We felt like two trees coming into leaf
watching the birth of procreative love.

God Glances at *The Life of Mammals*

May the young orangutan with small orange ears in Sumatra think it is godlike and praise me.

Let the crab-eater seal pup suckling in Antarctica bless me for milk and waterproof fur.

May the armies of succulent caterpillars munching their way through the aerial pastures be oblivious to their predators and pay lip-service to their great Provider.

May the European red squirrel jumping from conifer branch to conifer branch confirm that God is also a sacred acrobat.

Let the brown coati in Costa Rica with its mobile nose smell out its meals of fruit and lizards, mice and spiders, millipedes and nestling birds and give thanks for such delicious creepy-crawlies and biodiversity.

Let elephants tusking for salt in the caves of Mount Elgon, Kenya, give thanks for nutritious chemicals and an omnivorous memory.

May the dozing three-toed sloth hooked upside-down to a branch in South America dream a three-toed god in the cornucopia of its sleep.

Let the brown lemming emerging from its burrow in the rapid spring of the Canadian arctic extol my rotation of seasons.

May the heart of the pigmy shrew beating 1200 times per minute thump its little drum-beats in my honour.

The golden lion tamarin of South-east Brazil has a coat of pure red-gold like the skin of a sun-god in my image.

Let the male howler monkey calling in Costa Rica sing the praises of his howler monkey god. I too like a good howl.

May the Virginia opossum hanging by its long hairless prehensile tail from a tree branch in Florida bless the breeder of flora and fauna and the thirteen teats for its thirteen young.

The pygmy shrew eating three times its bodyweight in a diet of earthworms squeaks in inaudible homage to the providential supplier of vermiform life and edible insects.

May the striped tenrec of Madagascar vibrate its neck quills and squeal its rattling calls in ultrasonic praise of its deity.

Let the jaguar cat fishing above its own duplicitous reflection on a tributary of the Amazon find the fish it is waiting for.

May the sea otter with a million follicles per square inch of fur scoop out the crabmeat from a crabshell, using its furry stomach as both table and anvil, and thank the god of oceans for edible crustaceans.

May the epauletted fruitbat feeding on figs in West Africa scatter the seeds of my fig-trees in its excreta.

The gigantic blue whale surfacing in Baja California is spouting a geyser out of its blowhole in a psalm to the god of all waters. A blue whale's tongue is as big as an elephant, though neither of them be cognizant of this lingual fact.

May all my mammals revere me, not like some distant reptilian ancestor, but as their omnipresent progenitor, the God of mammalian love.

And you, the endangering species, both deadly and mortal, the makers of images, admirers of selves, and all who think you may have created or destroyed me, praise the fertile imagination of the deathless mammal-maker and unmaker.

Enjoy these captive images of your short-lived hegemony.

I am not and will never be anthropomorphic.

The stars do not know Olbers' Paradox.

Blackbird at Dusk

Visible only as orange beak
and not so much for its dark physique,
a blackbird sits in a sycamore tree
and sings what it's like for him to be.

It sings of earth and sings of sky,
of water's depth and the fiery eye,
it sings for life and the love of leaves
as words rejoice and music grieves.

Credo

Let the stellar planisphere
Position stars throughout the year
In mobile orbit every hour
Around the earth's biotic flower.

Let the cirrostratus clouds
Sing hosannas in their shrouds,
Fire in the belly of the globe
Defy the icecap's frozen robe.

Let avalanche and waterfall
Perform the rites of burial,
Evaporate and reappear
As ocean rain and human tear.

Let forest nights and florid days
Photosynthesize their praise
For sun and sunlight to repeat
Mantras to the mantle's heat.

Reasons to Wake

Prunus. Kerria.
Cherry blossom everywhere.
Apple. Almond. Pear.

Waterboatmen skate,
denting the surface tension
with their tiny feet.

The purple iris
with its trinity of tongues
licks the warm breeze.

Ducks land on the lake
making an audible splash
in the almost dark.

The moth's antenna
is a half-feather eyebrow
on each tiny eye.

A dragonfly hangs
from the birch like a catkin
with transparent wings.

How do damselflies
mate on wings over water
in a perfect S ?

Heatwave on fresh fruit.
The bananas are wearing
tight leopard-skin suits.

Hot day, mid-August.
Floating seeds and flying ants
enjoy wanderlust.

Dandelion seed,
asterisk on a thermal,
relishes the ride.

The poppy seeds breed
in a wineglass pagoda
full of microdots.

A green hand-grenade
contains the tall cedar's seed
and cathedral shade.

Neurotic squirrel
in ritual panic prepares
nuts for burial.

Two grounded crane flies.
One is knitting its eyebrows,
the other its thighs.

Sheep crop the green ground,
eating their moving shadows
as the sun goes down.

Wave lassoes a rock,
rinses the suds from its hair,
then departs in shock.

Floods. There are drowned boats,
and seagulls grooming themselves
on the mooring-posts.

Mist and fog droppings
glisten on the evergreens
in wintry weepings.

The skeletal trees
watch in lakes of rainwater
their drowned images.

Between root and tree,
the willow's alter ego
shivers silently.

Frozen old-man's beard,
whiskers on the embankment
end another year.

In the morning mist,
ghostly horses eat grey grass,
each blade spooked with frost.

A break in the cloud
hones under gunmetal sky
a lake like a blade.

The sun's turning up
yellow and purple gas flames
in each crocus crop.

Brimstone yellows breed
one sunny April Fool's Day,
daffodils on speed.

On the paving stones
a snail has left its liquid
runes in dotted lines.

Birds and shadow birds
fly skywards into the sky.
Words and more than words.

Mute Swan

Treading an arrogant V in water,
I look at myself and my own image:
eye to eye with an orange beak,
a bird with aristocratic hauteur,
a beautiful and cantankerous face
on a pure white body and snake-like neck.
Preening myself, I drink the mirage
and its embodiment of grace.

I too can walk on water as I run
beating my widespread wingspan down the lake,
until on gentler currents I am airborne.
The holy Ghost may double as a dove
but I am more immaculate as a swan
and I too am a god when I make love.

Wasp

Where the hell's the fucking exit
from this bloody box of gloom?
seems to say the angry insect
in its waspish idiom.
Sees the light and then attacks it,
savagely monotonous.
Light behind the window tricks it
to reiterate its loss.
A timid biped tries to coax it
into freedom out of doom,
with a paper guides and pokes it,
death-wish flying round the room.
Climbs the malice of the glazing
in a fury of despair,
tiger-stripes of anger blazing,
entrance equals . . . *Exit*. Zoom!
Freedom. Independence. Air

Minutes

The minutes of the previous meeting
in lumpy pedestrian prose
were appraised and approved by bleating,
matters arising arose,

and the items on the agenda
verbosely came and went:
compromise fought surrender;
meaning clarified meant.

Is there any other business?
A whole lot more, he thought.
Why should we act like prisoners
when time is far too short?

We are free to use our talents.
We shall all too soon be dead.
Let's live and to hell with balance.
Shall we minute that? they said.

Let's all get wasted this minute.
Let's party into the night.
And as for the paperwork, bin it.
It's trivial trouble and trite.

Now is for loving and laughter,
Let fluids in friendship flow.
The minutes of matings hereafter
Are over wherever we go.

Horticulturalist

Disappointed with people
and in particular himself,
he fell in love in later life
with apple trees in blossom,
the root formations of deciduous lives,
municipal tulips and primulas,
the candied confections of pink cherry-trees,
the candelabra of horse-chestnuts,
sudden sky-blue lagoons of bluebells
in the beech woods each April spring,
the crisp japonica embers
against blue sky, pink-scented verbena,
the gorse and kerria
and the regular reappearances
of lilac and laburnum flowers,
delphiniums and foxgloves,
till even the people became
more personable and plant-like
and as for the plants and trees
they asked of him only that he should breathe
and then not even breath.

DAVID KENNEDY

(1941–2001)

A critic of lethal wit
and epigrammatic pith
on what he and others wrote,
a mild authority on
authoritarian spite,
what David Kennedy said
his friends can often quote:
'Polite middle-class girls?
Duncan, it must be hell.'
And 'Sounds like the slippery slope
to senior management.'

A gifted musical mind
with encyclopaedic recall
of opus number and phrase,
who sang with White Shoe Blues
a calypso in creole.
We remember as well
the acts of kindness done
for the old and put-upon,
the helpless and the weak,
the trimming of the hedge
or mowing of the lawn.

And another anecdote:
computer on the blink,
the novel he lost in space,
a fiction set in a school
entitled *Goats and Monkeys*;

over eighty thousand words
vanished – gone without trace.
'It's not as if someone's died,'
but he sounded unconvinced
and so began again,
rewrote the whole from scratch.

Inadequate in our praise,
we also recollect
his stoicism in illness,
the Interferon years,
the life and soul of the ward,
the lack of selfish pity
and dearth of self-regard.
Pate prematurely bald,
beady watchful eyes,
no care for what he wore,
all clothing being disguise.

He often joked he wrote
all for posterity now:
'I shall not come again.'
Wherever you are or not
in the agnostic night,
David, may you be free
from orthodoxy and pain,
and help us who survive
to wonder, laugh and grieve
at our absurdities
without you here alive.

Posidonio

We are driving back from Posidonio.
On a bend in the road,
a snake, a long snake, seems to be crossing.
We stop the Jeep to watch it
coil and uncoil slowly
winding its way across the tarmac.

Coming in the opposite direction,
a Greek man on a moped
is urging me to crush the snake.
I feign incomprehension
and watch it coil its vertebrae gradually
into the tinder-dry undergrowth and safety:
a near-death experience
under some chunky tyres.

The man takes off his helmet
and lectures me angrily in Greek
through the open window of the hired Suzuki.
He looks the more dangerous animal,
a hot red-faced high-blood-pressured ape,
vituperative and venomous.
So I play the dumb ignorant tourist
and then say *capisco*
though I don't.

Seed Head

In the Archaeological Museum
in Samos Town,
an ivory bead
from the tusk of a long-dead elephant
has been crafted into a replica
of a seedless seed head of a poppy
with its little roof and dotted lines
like a delicate amulet
to be offered to an extinct goddess
and now in an airtight box
it stands with other artefacts
and terracotta figurines
in a room with a guard
doing the crossword
on a windowledge.
In the open air,
generations of poppies
seed themselves carelessly
year after year.

Day-Trip

We were on board the Samos Sky returning
from a day-trip to Turkey. Passports, water, icecream,
then up on deck enjoying air again
and travelling back at fourteen knots or so,
spray in our faces and sun on our heads,
sunglasses for the dazzle of the waves,
the sea-breeze in our hair, while salty crystals
dried quickly on the lenses of dark glasses.
Tired from a day at Ephesus in the heat
and journeying across its silted harbour,
a plain now with the Meander miles away.
The Atlas fountain by the Emperor Hadrian
dry as a bone, the amphitheatre's bowl,
the library and its attendant brothel,
all seen in noonday heat and packed with tourists,
the whirling dervishes of Turkish carpets
for sale in a display of national craft:
the tree of life and paradise in patterns.
Then suddenly we saw. A Dane stood up.
He pointed out and shouted look in Danish.
A dolphin leaping like itself, a dolphin,
its dark curve muscled unmistakably,
an outline arced from nose to tail to dorsal,
a wave embodied in a streamlined wave,
the archetypal mythic mammal-fish.
After the words and images it was real.
The captain slowed the boat to view the creature
Which leapt across our bows and vanished under
into its world of submarine evasions.
I knew that if I kept the starboard watch
the long-desired epiphany would happen.

Do Not Disturb

I'm feeling old, exhausted, tired and fat.
Give me a well-earned break. Donate me rest.
Castrate the telephone and hide the bell.
Bring me a tray of alcoholic drinks.
I need to convalesce in an hotel
And since I'm stultified and overstressed
I want to channel-trawl, take eighty winks
And veg out like a geriatric cat.

I know you know the feeling, Lord, because
You made the world, the universe, the moon,
The sun, the earth and all that therein was,
Like mountains, dinosaurs and early man,
In six days flat, then sat down on Day 7
To put your feet up on a chair in heaven.

Decent Citizen

It's so damn awkward being British
Although my passport says I am,
Born Oxford, 1947.
Well, maybe I am Anglo-Scottish.
How do I seem to you, my man?
So sorry. Ladies, gentlemen.
A vaguely bookish, Rupert Brookeish
Anachronistic English gent
Safe beneath his English heaven
Of fashionably mixed descent,
Urbane, ironic, wry and skittish?
Or another inhibited Englishman
Inhabited by a Caliban
Who wished he didn't give a damn?

Theory

In our Greco-Roman youth
We believed in love and truth.
In post-modernist decline
Signifier questions sign.

September Birthdays

I am becoming more like my father every day.
I even sound and yawn like him and on occasions
our quiet incursions into yesterday
which we call memory deceive me into thinking
I am not dead but he is living through me.
When tidying myself up in small doses
or watching a bottle-green fly on a flint stone
going about its business, I wonder who I am or was
and the brain-damaged moon has forgotten its name
and has nothing of great importance yet to say.
The shadows of the trees stretch in gradual elastications
towards evening as if imploring water
for their thirsts. They are prepared
to take our exhalations for their sustenance.
The powder thrown up by ants between the paving stones
is like our own detritus but more purposeful.
The smell of a melon ripening in a room
dispels the wintry melancholy of summer
approaching autumn yet again and its September birthdays.

Hymn to Pimm's

Dice the cucumber,
slice the lemon,
core and cube the apples,
add chopped oranges plus rind,
then pick a sprig or three of spearmint,
add translucent cubes of ice
and fizzy lemonade
to the sombre-looking liquid
the colour of varnish
but sniff the herbal
vermouth aroma
and taste the best of summer
from a glass jug's cornucopia
of sunlight, foliage and fruit,
enjoy the beatific vision,
the boozy snooze in a deckchair
on the lawn
and the headaches of oblivion
all alcoholic afternoon.

In the Vendée. Remember?

A long straight road towards a town called Angles.
The low perspective and the vanishing point.
A marshy flatland with irrigation ditches,
covered with duckweed and with waterplants,
breeding mosquitoes eager for our blood,
and watermeadows where the cattle fed,
swishing their tails and ripping verdant grasses
long into sunset over the Atlantic.

A figure in the distance near a bridge
came gradually closer. He cast and cast
his line, then showed us what he fished for
with a piece of red flannel cloth as lure
on a four-point barb like a mini-anchor.
Watch. In the dusk light of the ditch
frogs were deceived when they saw something move
and so they leapt as at a fly or some such
delicacy only to be impaled
on one of the four barbs. The Frenchman
catching them at the rate of one a minute
showed us his haul in a plastic shopping bag:
a tangled mass of frogs on Judgement Day,
a glum conglomerate of eyes and legs.

Indoor Market

The smells of coffee, herb and spice
enter and mingle in the nose.

Eggs fill a basket to the brim
and olives soak in tubs of brine.

The leafy groves of lettuces
admire the sheaved asparagus.

Ripe oranges and cleansing lemons
carry abandoned leaves and stems.

Jars of honey and bottles of oil
blink messages of lucent guile.

The polished skins of aubergines
wear a deep magenta shine.

Thick cartwheels of aerated cheese
make cliffs of milky merchandise.

An octopus contorts itself
into a globe of tentacles.

A raw red rabbit keeps for luck
Fur slippers and white mittens on.

A sheep denuded of its skin
hangs from the question of a hook.

Leopard

It paces the barred space of its enclosure
waiting for antelope to maim and maul
before it felines for the jugular.

Or stretching out its tensile strength and claws,
it dozes in the sun with one eye open
and waits bone-idle for idolaters.

Sharp teeth surround the caverns of its yawns.
The eyeballs look aloof on distance till
distracted by the pigeons on the roof.

Faint sunlight glistens on its dappled pelt
of charcoal lozenges and tawny suede.
The tail is its perimeter of anger.

Inscrutable eyes in search of impetus,
it laps the sky and ripples its reflection
in the dull moat of constipated water.

A movement of bright fur on mobile bones,
it dreams of haunches on the wide savannahs
and wildcat couplings under dusty trees.

Tomorrow

From the beginning of the day
when sunrise shoots its arrow
until the remnants of the sky
in darkened charcoal narrow,
what is there left for me to say
in anger or in sorrow
and what's the purpose of today
if not to be tomorrow?

I talk myself to sleep at night
or cry into my pillow.
The world outside is cancelled light
and shadows lying fallow.
Why did you have to go away,
was there no time to borrow
and what's the purpose of today
or reason for tomorrow?

Though reassuring clichés say
that better times will follow,
tomorrow is another day
whose promises are hollow.
If you were god to you I'd pray
in anger and in sorrow
to give us back our yesterday
and recreate tomorrow.

Lycoperdon

A spherical
white puffball
has emerged
from the moss,
a little brain
half buried in grass
a new full moon
and satellite
of long-dead root,
a spongiform
bald cranium
humid tumour
and meringue
of fungal growth,
vegetable egg
and white leather purse
of ripening spores,
each ready to rule
the puffball earth
and universe.

History of Tom

I well remember Tom
as one of the Bash Street Kids,
his often cheerful grin
splitting that large round face,
not thirty but thirteen,

and later friend of daughter,
king of the barbecue,
bar-worker in New York,
broker of talk and laughter,
and practical joker too.

He often looked for work,
the secrets not revealed
across the ocean water
somewhere in idle talk
of married life that failed.

A mortal man and boy,
he could not bear to live
the sentence of slow death,
so he marked *The Prophet*'s page
at Sorrow and at Joy

and walked beyond the stage
into a public park,
selected a winter tree
and in the December wind
hanged himself in the dark.

What does the mind become
out of this world in time
when it takes itself beyond,
beyond the void mundane
into another void?

It's too late to repine
but penitent we bless.
We wish Tom Morley peace.
We wish his spirit rest
and everlasting grace.

All Saints

A cold wind from the east
blew seagulls inland
to where Canada geese
cornered the foreground
in front of the island,
Isleworth Ait,
where a heron landed
among leafless willows,
the mud-brown Thames
washed its tidal foreshore
and the cold east wind
dishevelled the water.

The mourners foregathered
by the Saxon tower
and the modern nave
of All Saints' Church.
Young men looked older,
thickened, hair thinning.
Relatives arrived
in sombre dark clothing,
recognised, spoke,
spoke of the sadness,
registered shock
while popular music
played his favourite songs.

Just after eleven
by the black and white clock
the hearse arrived
with a cross of flowers
over the coffin.
Sunlight threw patterns
on tall wooden columns.
The memories of Tom
and lost time flooded back
as the hymns were sung
for the young man who forsook
this living and us,
and the funeral address
by an eloquent friend
paid tribute in anecdote
to the Why and Why not
of the boy and the man.

After the blessing
the coffin was turned
and the family followed
the bearers and priest
out to cold sunlight
to the road and the river
which flows through the city
and out to the sea.

Anthropophily

Yes, I love you.
So let me introduce myself to you
in a high-pitched whine
as Mrs or Ms
Anopheles Mosquito.
I need a blood meal
for the breeding of my eggs.

Let me stand on your skin
in my arthropod stance
looking like an early biplane
and suck my emoluments
out of your blood supply.
I inoculate you while you sleep
and the parasites in my spittle
invade your liver.

What do I care if you die
so long as my eggs can wriggle
into a rainbow nation of larvae
in that contaminated puddle
and continue the line
Anopheline
into infinity?

Guilt

God looked
at the two hands
clasped in prayer.

He saw the fingers,
fingers and thumbs,
of a child-molester

asking forgiveness.
A psychologist,
he read the mind

as it confessed.
Forget it he thought.
You must take what comes.

That night God knelt
and asked forgiveness
of a broken child.

Telephone

For once
God picked up
the telephone.

His number
was ex-directory
given to no one.

He let it ring
three times before
he answered it.

He picked up
the receiver
and remained silent.

The voices
at the other end
sounded familiar,

sounded
like a younger version
of his own godhead.

He hoped
humanity had not
found him.

He listened to
praise abuse questions
hymns prayers sermons screams

birdsong rocksongs
accusations oceans
babble Babel drivel dreams,

all in
a nano-second or so
and then the line went dead.

International Gallery

J.W.M. Turner
had a nice little earner
putting water vapour
on canvas and paper.

Nobody supposes
Pablo Picasso
had four eyes
and two noses.

Mad Van Gogh
cut his ear off.
Vincent sad saint
bandaged it with paint.

Henri Matisse
loves colour and peace.
His *violon d'Ingres*
knows no anger.

Damien Hirst
had the first laugh
on the dead cow
he cut in half.

The eyes avoid
Lucien Freud.
Paint and flesh
look dead not fresh.

Gauguin Paul
sought Eden and all
in the South Seas.
Caught a disease.

Leonardo da Vinci
was a bastard, true.
Also a gay raunchy
left-handed genius too.

Edward Hopper
painted proper
portraits of loneliness
in the U.S.

Crippled in Mexico
Frida Kahlo
did you-know-what-ski
with exiled Trotsky.

For sexual relief
Georgia O'Keefe
painted the yoni
of poppy and peony.

Mrs Mahler's
easy lay,
Oscar Kokoschka
seems OK.

Sock it to me
David Hockney
loves pools and boys.
Big Splash. No noise.

In the world of Hogarth
ogres and gargoyles
roués and rakes
ogle and argue.
Innocence breaks.

Reason's slumbers
murder numbers.
Deaf old Goya
sees paranoia.

Ants in his pants,
Dali laughs,
melts a clock
and burns giraffes.

René Magritte
composes neat
mirrors of mysteries
without histories.

Even with rheumatism,
brush tied to his hand,
old Renoir enjoyed nudism
to gladden the gland.

Protuberance and exuberance.
Sir Peter Paul Rubens
has got the hots
for Flemish fleshpots.

Wriggle squiggle red blue yellow,
What do you think you are, old fellow?
Miró, Miró, on the wall
are you a microbe after all?

Winslow Homer
was a roamer.
Painted the seaboard himself
from North to Gulf.

Society Sargent
could handle paint
but a modern Van Dyck
he probably ain't.

It's all right to stare
at the Folies-Bergère
but picnicking nude
is thought lewd and crude.
Beware, Edouard Manet, beware.

While his wife drowns in the bath
Pierre Bonnard
plays possum
in the apple and almond blossom.

Howard Hodgkin
makes a splodgkin.
Memory's colours
seem a solace.

Kitschy Koons
plays Disney tunes.
Dealers cash in on
media fashion.

Louise Bourgeois
recreates Kafka's
imaginary
menagerie.

Not simply fey,
Paul Klee
daydreams lines and pigments
into signs and figments.

Making hay
while the sun shone
on the lilypond
is what Monet
has been and done
in the blue yonder and beyond.

When both he and the pooch
needed an outing,
Pieter de Hooch
painted tiles and grouting.

Girl with a hula hoop,
would you like to meet
Giorgio di Chirico
in a darkened street?

Most painted mountain?
Mt Ste. Victoire.
The man Cézanne.
La France la gloire.

Seurat stipples
water with dots.
Lots and lots and lots
make ripples.

Munch's scream
was more than a yelp:
a universal
cry for help.

Eschewing green,
Mondrian stares
at oblongs and squares
but what they mean
nobody cares.

The complaint
about Nicolas Poussin should be
that he's Milton in paint.
(Nick Chicken N.B.)

Sex obsesses
brilliant youth.
Egon Schiele
tells the truth.

Lucio Fontana
stabbed and ripped.
Jackson Pollock
dipped and dripped.

After they have had a barney
and she is pregnant – yet to learn –
tubercular Modigliani
beatifies Jeanne Hébuterne.

Life looked blacker
when Marc and Macke
met their maker
and attacker.

Honoré Daumier
what a sharp mind
called it a day
when he went blind.

SHERIFF OF WASHINGTON

I'm George the Unelected
But thanks to brother Jeb
Here I am in the White House
And on the world wide web.

Ex-Governor of Texas,
My money is in oil,
So pay back all the taxes
And take Iraqi soil.

I will not sign a treaty
Which cuts down poison gas.
I can tell good from evil,
My assets from my ass.

The Sheriff now of Washington,
I talk like Wyatt Earp.
The Dubya stands for Wal-Mart,
The President for twerp.

I been to Yale and Harvard
And though I cannot spell
Thanks to the good Lord Jesus
I'm anti-infidel.

So God the Father help me,
God help me Daddy Bush.
Let's all go give this Middle East
A god-almighty push.

Weapons of mass-destruction
Paraded on the streets.
What proof Saddam has gottem?
We kept goddam receipts.

Tell anyone who deniggerates
As stupid rich white trash
The President of the United States
I paid for it in cash.

                        April, 2003

Sir John Betjeman Turns in His Grave

Come, Concorde jet, and crash on Reading,
Prevent suburbia from spreading,
Obliterate with delta wing
The Inner Distribution Ring.

Come noisiest jet that's ever flown,
Wreck county town with flaming stone,
Reduce to rubble's concrete rocks
Both Toys "Я" Us and Knickerbox.

Let the gasometers explode
Near Tesco's store on Napier Road.
Both Reading Gaol and Apex Plaza
Beg to be *tabula* and *rasa*.

Let all the traffic jams be gone
From Winnersh to the Hexagon.
Clear up the mess of Reading Station
With unannounced annihilation.

And as the metal phoenix dies
Let fossil fuels light up the skies
But save the passengers and crew
With something that a psychic knew.

Give certain people clear forewarning
Not to go shopping on that morning.
Prolong the Royal Berks' existence.
Spare Blackwells and its kind assistants.

Come supersonic bird of prey,
Fall to the ground and make my day.
Huntley & Palmers, Courage Beer
And Sutton's Seeds once flourished here.

Let's start again with blue-sky thinking,
With watermeadows, cattle drinking
And, set among these natural gems,
The unadulterated Thames.

Risk Assessment

What do we do when we risk assess?
We have a look and take a guess.
We use our well-known second sight
To prevent débâcles before tonight.
So what does the weather forecaster say?
Are storms and hurricanes on the way?
Has the coach been checked for every mile
And is it driven by a speedophile?
Have you got money, a mobile phone,
A rape alarm and a funny bone?
Told an adult where you are going?
Know what you're doing and/or knowing?
Thought about pregnancy on the bus?
Joining the Natural Childbirth Trust?
Have you got water, food and drink?
Are all chronometers now in sync?
Have you a photograph of your face
And what's your number just in case?
What is your worst case film scenario?
Double the damage and think in stereo.
Estimate your time of arrival,
The party's chances of survival,
Your odds against the forces of evil,
The body's failure, mind's upheaval,
And what if you have a panic attack?
You're having one now! Oh God! Step back.

Autumn Again

Today the starlings have started to foregather.
They are electing whether to migrate
in noisy parliaments of beak and feather
or in their flocks of syncopated flight.
And on the single lime tree where they natter
the leaves are fading early, yellow, brown.
Another few have fallen in a litter
of drying individuals on the ground.
The starlings add their vocal animation
and antics to the stillness of the lime,
the patterns of the growth rings and migration
are both defying death and killing time
while by releasing seeds into the air
the willowherb presumes another year.

Brown Dragonfly

A big brown dragonfly whirs
from the Triassic era
into the garden here.

It dominates the air
bringing an insect terror
into a summer hour,

imagining it were
not a voracious larva
breeding year by year

but the gunship flower
of winged immortal warrior
breathing dragon fire.

Toad

Pick him up and he's
a piss-artist out of nappies.
Look at the juice he pees,
terrified of being eaten.

Pulsing panicky dewlap
of double chin,
a stuffed vineleaf,
all mouth and trousers,
he paddles the air
in vain with
inedible thighs
and flipper forepaws.

Amphibious lung
with large malevolent
unblinking eyes,
an obese squat lizard,
discoloured and verrucous,
camouflaged as mud,
slime-green leafmould
or khaki turd.

Jumping genitalia!
Off he goes
to fertilize the ropes
of little toads.

Bubbly

Open the bottle of fizz
remove the golden foil
around the suggestive shape
untwist the chinstrap wire
doff the metallic casque
and slowly withdraw the cork
pop the champagne and pour
into the glass or flute
and down the hatch or the throat
alcohol fills the veins
convivial trivial jokes
trip off the loosened tongue
juices of girls' and blokes'
appetites start to sing,
the drug in the jug delights,
half a carafe is a laugh
and the greatest of the apes
is rabbiting like a god
as inhibitions fade
and appetites increase
all things are possible
and everyone's on the pull
before the thirst in the night
the ache in the throbbing head
and the yawning morning sight
of bubbles down the pan.

Sex Romp in Head's Garden

Go near it and they lie doggo
but watch it through the window
and the frog pond is winking, jerking,
blinking in a frenzied froggy orgy
of mating, coupling, amphibian bubbles,
fertilising eggs, frogspawn and frigspunk.
The waterline is seething and on the surface floats
a tapioca island of globular frogspawn.

Even the Manx cat stops to watch
all those frigging ignoramuses
in a group-sex spectacular of amphibious rogering,
a fizzing oblong of fornicating frogs,
an extrusion of juices in a jacuzzi.

Hearing my heavy footsteps,
they freeze as at a police raid,
lying legs akimbo on their backs
in attitudes of innocent exhaustion.

Their future lies congealed above their heads,
gelatinous and ignorant in cells.

Flight

(MH 0133)

Take off from Kuala Lumpur.
The temperature outside is minus 60.
We're somewhere over the Equator
and I'm in love. Desire on sight.
You're modelling
a Malaysian airlines dress
of floral purple, green and mauve
where lotus stems and flowers intertwine.
We're nearly six miles high,
more than 4,000 miles from Mecca.
With film star looks
and movie ease of movement,
wasp-waist and nubile hips
accentuated by the uniform,
ankle-length but figure-hugging,
you are a people-person obviously.
Your name badge calls you FAZIAN
but how do you pronounce it?
I expect to see you soon on DVD
or on the video screen in front of me.
Our ground speed is 666 miles per hour.
The clouds outside are blushing chiffon pink.
You bring a meal and your professional smile
seems perfect orthodontically and real.
Your eye shadow's an opalescent mauve.
Don't move. I want to memorise your profile.
Could this be love?
The Great Dividing Range seen from above?
Emerging from a curtain of blue pleats,
you bring us ice-cold orange juice to drink.
Red wine or white? Your golden arms provide

a breast of chicken flying six miles high.
We're somewhere over Coober Peedy now.
Goodbye, dear Fazian, goodbye.
And happy landings, Madam Butterfly.

God

Who will believe you
after humanity?
who will revile you
as a nonentity?
who will extol you
into infinity?
who will obey you
like an enemy?
who will betray you
as a friend?

Without mankind no God.
Without God no humanity.
Without humanity
world without end.

FRIDAY NIGHT WITH JONATHAN ROSS

It's probably preserved on videotape
in the piracy of various homes
or in the archives of the BBC:
Sir David Attenborough on
Friday Night With Jonathan Ross,
two very different types of Englishman.
Foppish yob from Leytonstone leans forward
in a stripy suit and says,
'So, Sir David, I'm a gweat admiwer
of all your wild life pwogwammes, have been for years,
I watched your bwavery with gowillas and all that,
learnt a lot, had a good laugh.
You're a much twavelled man.
What have you learnt after a lifetime of study
in the natural world?'

Senior citizen, fluffy-haired, blue-shirted gent
says, 'Well, I've learnt that if you
took away the entire human race tomorrow,
it would make no difference whatsoever
to the rest of the planet.'

Pause. Long pause.
Homo verbosus lost for words.

Sloe Gin

The taste reminds me
of being young again.
The stained-glass thimbleful
of purple liquid
is sweet and pungent on the tongue
and the taste is not of plums
but wild blackthorn fruit
picked mature from hedgerows
after the first frosts of autumn.

I am in my grandmother's house.
I have in my hand a glass
of her home-made sloe gin
and we are listening
to Paul Robeson sing
on a wind-up gramophone
as big as a pulpit
while I at eight or nine
am certain what it will be
to feel grown up.

Sloe gin and Old Man River.
The bushes have flowered
and petals fallen
for half a century since then.

Window Seat

Lucky to see the Alps the other day.
Clouds parted and the mountains brown and white
Revealed themselves in a romantic way
Stagelit by rosy rays of sunset light
And on my lap an unromantic tray
Of microwaved fast Flying Colours food:
Braised Beef with Dumpling, not that I can moan
At complimentary drinks of Chilean red.
No in-flight entertainment, thank the Lord.
Next, coffee and a Mini Toblerone
Not far from where the chocolate was invented.
And then a lake which I thought Bodensee . . .
I watched the world go by in Godlike mood
Like you in *Genesis* and it was good.

8 October

Crouched under
the chestnuts
like a voyeur
I watched it all
in the sunlight.

The copulating wasps,
he courting her,
wings aquiver,
the triangular head
and black tongue

licking her ovipositer
in unmistakeable pleasure,
the two united by the tail
in a waspish S
of frenzied stillness.

Winter Weather

The deepening gloom
of a British Sunday afternoon in late December
has to be seen to be imagined.
Wood pigeons and squirrels
are the embodiments of grey and damp.

A flock of seagulls
blown inland against a rainy sky
forages for nothing.
A diesel engine lows beside the station
and the bare branches drip
deciduous raindrops into sedentary puddles
over drains.

The mistletoe hangs far too high for lovers
and we tape-record our favourite tracks
or label photographs of a forgotten summer
in an album
by electric light.

August Bank Holiday

It has been a bank holiday Monday,
a day of ineluctable melancholy.
The summer's over and the summer of our lives.
The children have gone returning to their rented properties.
I get through the day without self-harming
and without lacerating my past selves for producing the future.
It has been a good day on the whole, melancholia
   notwithstanding.

The tilt of the globe towards autumn
is almost palpable in the atmosphere.
Leaves look as if they are about to detach themselves
and fulfil an alternative purpose.
The buddleia shivers in the late August wind.

It felt like a Sunday after Sunday lunchtime
and we were all four conscious of departures.
The children's games were in the hall awaiting
their free delivery to the charity shop:
Cluedo, Pyk-a-Styk and The Game of Life.

Struthio

I tried to start an ostrich farm,
To sell the meat to restaurants,
With profits to the power of n
Fit for a supermarket chain.
I kept them in a heated barn,
A shed of ostriches all day
Which wanted food. Inspectors came.

The eggs had failed to incubate
And birds to breed. I felt to blame
And grew to loathe the pungent smells
Of rubber necks and massive feet,
Their feeding-times and flock-togethers,
The giant eggs and tiny heads,
Their scaly legs and grubby feathers.

I searched for formulae of words
And fellow victims of the scam
To sell the flightless flock of birds,
Uprooted from their southern home.
As if they had some right to preach,
The birds looked puzzled and aloof.

I dreamed of races on the beach
Where massive poultry on the hoof
Could plant their baby heads in sand
And I could drown myself inland
And re-emerge as someone else.

Tonight

Tonight I am too tired for an emotion,
too tired for stimulus or animation,
too tired to cross the garden or the ocean,
too tired for semiotic information.
Tonight I have abandoned all ambition,
it's time to undermine determination,
I've thrown away the key to the ignition,
don't bother me with any delegation.
Tonight I have no time for erudition,
for introspection or for cerebration,
it's time to celebrate my manumission
from friction, fashion, fusion and frustration.
My digits do not want to be remastered,
says past-it bastard asking to get plastered.

Sleep

Weary with waking and working week-in and week-out,
Moving mountainous molehills of mutinous mud,
The body, the brain and bones are begging for bed.
Warm as the womb the welcoming wimples wait,
Pillows appeal, piled into pairs and plump,
A heated home for the heavy hedonist head.
Mattress's metal and man-made materials
Mould the movement and meat of mammal and mate,
Nudists nesting in night's negation of now.
The limbs in limbo, liberty languages live,
Dreamland's derivative dramas delight and distress,
Soap-opera selves survive surrealist scenes,
Released from routine and refreshed by ritual rest.
Oh this is the life if this is the life after death.

God in the Small Hours

I too wake in the small hours
and think dark thoughts of my own devising.
Remember I do not have your
devious devices and desires
which some of your compatriots
and others confess to me
and I find predictably diverting.
I cannot drink a glass or two of wine
or fantasise about my sexual partners,
past and future, real or imagined,
or worry about money
or whether I shall ever be a grandparent.
Eternity is a long time to contemplate
and does not induce any sense of urgency.
I too remember my mistakes,
catastrophes and aberrations
but I do not have dreams to distract me
or death to defy.

Patriarch

It's time I recreated
the womanhood
of the godhead
she's had a bad press
God said
and was as good
as his word.

A transformation,
a transfiguration,
a transmogrification occurred
and he re-emerged
not as a mere cross-dresser
with feminist empathies
nor a mother confessor
but as a new role-model.
Nothing stereotypical.
No feminine freak or fake.

God what a gorgeous apple,
She said. God what a sexy snake!

Outlook

What am I now,
now that I'm old?

Who was I then
when I was young?

What will I be
when dead and cold?

Where have I been
both old and young?

And in between
where has it gone?

What have I been,
all said and done?

What does it mean,
oblivion?

Typography

A morning glory opening at noon,
Intensest lapis blue of lazuli,
The turquoise swimming pool of a lagoon,
Grey willows in a watermeadow green,
Gold pollen dust of daffodils in spring,
Vermilion poppies in a field of grain,
Bright yellow lemons, biscuit brown of loaves,
The pink and purple dawn of ingot orange,
The dying ember flames of autumn leaves,
The berry red, the blood in the syringe:
The words are black on white but close your eyes
On any hymn to daylight and delight
And what if vision of the vision dies?
The sky is paper and the words are night.

Magpie

A garden drama. Just now.
I set it down as it happened.
A magpie had dumped a fledgling on the ground
and was pecking its innards out.
Alarmed, both male and female blackbird
made daring frantic passes over
and round the magpie but to no avail.
On the grass below
mauve and white lilac bushes,
the nestling's feet pedalled the air.
Brown hen and black cock fluttered and watched
as the magpie extracted
a round red thing, a globule of protein,
and flew away with the heart.
Then returned to pluck the fledgling
and enjoy another warm meal.
It came back to finish the job
like a killer whale.
And now the cradle-snatched husk
lies upside-down on the lawn
and the blackbirds return
to their responsibilities
with rain and sunset coming on.

In the Cupboard

Over the summer
a ginger root
has grown in the dark
a bright green shoot.

So I plant it out
to see what will grow
and water the earth
and as I do

I remember making
ginger beer
from a recipe as
a nine-year-old

and the ginger beer plant
in the Kilner jar:
yeast and ground ginger
fed with white sugar,

its lunar eruptions
and solar flares,
its bubbles and stir
and the bottles of beer

my mother tended
with daily care
and the fizz we drank
in '56.

I would love some now,
some ginger beer,
in memoriam
Dad and her.

Mother and Daughter

First you were time and then the bomb,
The other woman in the room.

You were the miracle we begot,
The open secret in the cot.

I am the purse which subsidized
The tears you shed and dried your eyes.

I was the mentor who discussed
Endless dilemmas on your quest.

As mother of a teenage child,
I was the costume you reviled.

Similar tune but different song
Reminds me now of being young.

You were the woman in my womb.
She is the future that I am.

An Odyssey

My long-planned film of *The Odyssey*
says less about Homer than about me.
Money no object. I produce.
Paul Newman has signed on as Zeus.
Poseidon is Robert Redford please.
Hephaistos? Brian Blessed agrees.
Wily Odysseus would have been
Sean Connery in his James Bond prime
but we are looking for an unknown
for all those journeys, sails and oars,
island sirens, foreign shores.
Schwarzenegger is Polyphemus.
This odyssey is polysemous;
the sirens are many and various.
Name your favourite enchantresses,
chanteuse, diva, nymph or goddess.
Computer graphics and special effects
create a vortex and clashing rocks.
The Mediterranean locations
provide the crew with divagations.
Suitors for Penelope include
Richard Gere and that Crowe dude,
William Clinton and John Travolta,
The faithful hound is Scoobydoo
and Telemachus? Well. Orlando who?
Al Pacino and all have tried
to draw the monstrous bow and failed;
So I show up and pull the string,
I turn the bow on the whole bang fling
And find Penelope is you
Older, wiser and wrinkled too.

Tanga

Looked like underpants but more so
judging from the pictured torso.
Got my tanga on me now,
rather tight from stern to prow,
tighter than a thong from Tonga,
wish its arms and legs were longer.

Need to be a slimmer swimmer
to tango in this Tesco's tanga,
tangle with the jet-black jockstrap,
strangulating cotton mantrap.
Wish were better hung and younger
when I bought them for a song,
had no inkling when was tinkling
I'd be throttled by a thong.

Looked the word up, eeny-meeny,
'type of very brief bikini',
gives my brief-case other meaning,
breathe in now for paunchy preening.
Half-price bargain tempts a shopper,
now no longer teenybopper
but a grumpy 50 something,
likes home comforts round his whatsit
not a loin-cloth up his coccyx.

Fashion victim inadvertent
not by boxer shorts am curtained
but by tangas left *al fresco*.
Never underpant at Tesco.

Mirror, mirror on the wall
told me pride preceded fall.
Silly me. I'm hardly broke.
Caveat emptor. Pig in poke.
Ponderous buttock, waist-high thigh.
Careful owner, much confused.
Anybody like to buy
six black tangas barely used?

Denial

This is a happy poem,
it does not mention death,
it loves its happy home
with every jolly breath.

It does not rue the day,
it does not dread the night,
it says hip-hip-hooray
mankind has got it right.

It's so affirmative
it says a jumbo yes,
how wonderful to live!
Amen. Hoorah. God bless.

So eat up, drink, be merry.
Sing women, wine and song.
This life is joyful, very,
and nothing can go wrong.

Praise be for love and sex
for they are both the same.
There are no nervous wrecks
where mating is the game.

The body is not ridden
by fever or disease.
The mind is not a midden
whose images displease.

The conscience is not governed
by scruples or by qualms.
There is no clique nor coven
and evil never harms.

Garden Leave

Sitting here in the warm
I like so much to hear
the birdsong and their talk
enter the inner ear.
The dandelion on the lawn
under my deck-chaired bum
is desperate to produce
a dandelion clock
so that its seed may swarm
and release another wave
of sunlit replicas
out of the fertile earth
as if all purpose were
creation and rebirth.

Gifts

Tulips and orchids
orchids and tulips
each of them gifts
and gifts in themselves.

The orchids from Thailand
magenta and white
the tulips from Holland
white and cerise.

Sitting room tulips
and orchid front hall
perfume the rooms
with a flourishing smile.

Forget about breath
and fossil fuel
ignore the deaths
cut flowers entail.

Think of them now
as beautiful
think of it all
as gifts for a while.

Round

Had we foreseen with hindsight's gift,
Had we foreknowledge of the past,
Had we foretold before the start,
If we could have our time again,
Had we but known the work entailed,
If premonitions could alarm,

No life's ambition would have failed,
None of our loved ones come to harm,
Rejuvenated we could then
Prevent the fractures of the heart,
Rewrite the storylines and cast,
Had we but once foreknown the drift.

Sands

Come unto these yellow sands
but are they really yellow though?
Run the granules through your hands
or stir the powder with your toe,
some glimmer like a mirror's shards,
some black as night or white as snow
under the galaxies of stars
where oceans move and mountains grow
to evolution's random plans
whose mills may grind exceeding slow
though nobody yet understands
those origins of long ago.
Come unto these fallow sands
and see what wildernesses know.

Mystic

The visions of the visionary
Are versions to the mind
Averse to myth and mystery,
By misery made blind.

From years of desperation's
Undiagnosed malaise
I turned to meditation
To sanctify my days.

Clairvoyant I saw paradise
And colonies of death.
I saw the Christ they sacrificed
And Buddha's prana breath.

To some I seem a fantasist,
To some perhaps deranged,
But in those moments I exist
And by them I was changed.

Vision

Look at the bumble bee on lavender,
The fuchsia with its ballerina flowers,
Picture the swallows as they drink from water,
The morning glory in its open hours,
Regard the water's dance of mural lights
Wandering on the wall and, out to sea,
The sky reflecting planetary blue
As delicate as an eyeball and in orbit,
And then give thanks for eyesight and confess
That self-regard is nothing where the world
Gives visions of miraculous loveliness
Which would be blurred and bleary in the wild,
Till you fear blindness more than any loss
Before the end of all and eyelessness.

Whodunnit

Who killed the deity?
I said the atheist
with my impiety.

Who destroyed numen?
I said the criminal,
crime being human.

Who told the truth?
I said the paragraph
once in my youth.

Who buried evidence?
I said the conscience,
deep in irrelevance.

Who'll stand on trial?
I said denial,
plotting betrayal.

Whose is the vengeance?
Mine say the engines
in prisons and dungeons.

Who cancelled the past?
I the iconoclast
denuded it fast.

Who betrayed ignorance?
We said the parents
with our forbearance.

Who did you doubt?
Ourselves said the clouds
shaping incertitudes.

Who stole the daylight?
I said the night
for my darkest delight.

Whodunnit and why?
I said eternity
unable to die.

Full Circle

When forests breathe
and fibres drink
they preconceive
no printer's ink

Inside the rings
of growing bark
we speak our lives
against the dark

Long afterwards
foul papers know
two singing birds
on vanished snow